THEY WALK THE EARTH

THEY WALK THE

The Extraordinary Travels of Animals on Land

EARTH

by **Seymour Simon**   *Illustrated by* **Elsa Warnick**

BROWNDEER PRESS • HARCOURT, INC. • SAN DIEGO • NEW YORK • LONDON

Requests for permission to make copies of any part of the work should be mailed to:
Permissions Department, Harcourt, Inc., 6277 Sea Harbor Drive, Orlando, Florida 32887-6777.

Browndeer Press is a registered trademark of Harcourt, Inc.

Library of Congress Cataloging-in-Publication Data
Simon, Seymour.
They walk the earth: the extraordinary travels of animals on land/Seymour Simon;
illustrated by Elsa Warnick.
p.   cm.
"Browndeer Press."
Summary: Describes the movement and migration of mammals and amphibians over varying
conditions of land, covering such species as lemmings, elephants, caribou, and frogs.
1. Mammals—Migration—Juvenile literature.   2. Amphibians—Migration—Juvenile literature.
[1. Animals—Migration.]   I. Warnick, Elsa, ill.   II. Title.
QL739.5.S56   2000
599.156´8—dc21   98-38732
ISBN 0-15-292889-8

First edition
F E D C B A
PRINTED IN HONG KONG

JQ
591.568
Simon

To Joel, Benjamin, Chloe, and Jeremy,
my grandchildren, with love
—S. S.

For Martha
—E. W.

*I*n one way or another, land animals, small and large, are always on the move. While many animals walk the earth only around their birthplaces, others go on long seasonal journeys called migrations. Animals migrate in order to survive when the weather becomes too hot or too cold, or when food becomes scarce or unavailable.

Every spring and summer, frogs and toads hop and jump their way across fields, meadows, swamps, and roads in search of water in which to spawn. Caribou tirelessly push across snow-covered lands for thousands of miles each year in search of food.

Lemmings—small rodents about the size of a fist—also go on journeys every year. But once every thirty years or so, huge numbers of Norwegian lemmings pour down from their homes in the mountains toward a distant sea, where they plunge in and drown by the thousands.

Ever-changing clouds of animals travel across the grasslands of East Africa in a yearly nineteen-hundred-mile trek. Herds of a million or more wildebeests and thousands of zebras and gazelles search for food and water together. Lions, leopards, and hyenas follow the herds, preying upon the journeying grass eaters. Looking like the shadows of hills upon the African landscape, elephants also roam long distances in search of their daily needs of food and of water.

Humans are perhaps the greatest voyagers of all. Early peoples were nomads. They traveled across the lands they lived on, and with boats they journeyed across the seas. Even in our modern age, people travel to other lands as immigrants, hoping to find a better life for themselves and their children. As we begin to travel in space, new migrations may take place: to colonies on the moon, on Mars, and perhaps on even more distant planets in other solar systems.

All these land journeys take place in a host of different surroundings: snow-covered, icy steppes; shifting golden desert sands; humid and dripping tropical rain forests; misty mountains; endless miles of waving grasslands; soggy wetlands; and many combinations of these.

Mammals are the most common migrants on land. Cold-weather mammals usually have protective fur coats and can store fat in their bodies as energy reserves. Desert mammals can store water and have ways to protect themselves against excessive heat. And mammals that are constantly on the move have hooves or paws or claws that allow them to move easily for long distances over snow or sand or mud.

Some animals, such as caribou, travel almost all year long. Others, such as the elephant and the polar bear, travel far only when food supplies run short and they need to move on.

Caribou are wild reindeer, the same kind of animals that are pictured pulling Santa Claus's Christmas sled. (The species is known as "caribou" in North America and "reindeer" in Scandinavia and Siberia.) Barren-ground caribou live in the harsh climate of northern Alaska and Canada.

Movement is the key to the barren-ground caribou's survival. They must search for food in stark surroundings that change dramatically with the seasons. During most of the year, the caribou eat lichens and mosses. But these foods contain very few of the proteins and minerals that mothers need to produce milk for their young calves. So during the summer, the caribou travel for many miles across the tundra to find green plants that contain these nutrients. Wolves and grizzly bears, which might threaten their young, are less plentiful on these summer ranges.

Most caribou herds travel along the same paths that earlier herds have taken in previous years. Caribou migrations begin in the spring, when the herds journey from their wintering grounds in the forested lands of southern Canada to the plains of the Alaskan tundra, hundreds of miles to the north. The first to leave are female caribou, heavy with their unborn young. They begin their long trek when the southern forests are still covered with snow and arrive when the northern tundra is still frozen and hard. The journey takes about a month. In the north they will give birth to their young and eat the new grasses that grow in the spring.

Recently a dozen female caribou were tracked by satellite and were found to travel incredibly huge distances. One female traveled more than 3,100 miles in a year, the greatest distance ever recorded for a land animal. It is an extraordinary feat considering it was accomplished without maps or roads and highways.

Migrating caribou tend to move more easily across icy places such as frozen lakes and windswept ridges where the snow is hard. If a herd encounters a very deep snowdrift, the caribou travel single file, usually led by an adult female who breaks a trail through the snow. After a mile or so, another caribou will take the lead.

Caribou are well adapted for their long, cold journey. Sometimes called "the camels of the frozen north," caribou have broad hooves that spread wide when they walk across the snow. They also can paw away the snow to get at their main food, the mosses and lichens growing underneath. Caribou are protected against the cold by their warm fur.

Caribou march slowly along at two or three miles per hour, feeding on lichens and dried leaves as they walk. Every few hours the animals rest for an hour or two. If another group of caribou walks by, some of the resting animals may stand up and join that group to continue their journey. Caribou travel both during the day and at night.

Once the caribou reach the barren grounds of the tundra, the large groups break up into smaller ones that travel in different directions. Caribou cows often give birth alone, because they have to stop while the rest of the herd keeps moving. For a week or ten days after calving, the cow and her calf remain in the same area, searching for new grasses.

Soon the mother and her calf join others. Small herds of mothers and their calves form and grow larger. Within two weeks of calving, the caribou are again traveling together. Now males—called bulls—and females without offspring join the cows and their calves.

Barren-ground caribou travel more during the summer months than at any other time of the year, mostly to avoid the mosquitoes and flies that are plentiful then. The caribou travel to the seacoasts of the Arctic and to high mountain ridges, where breezes and cooler temperatures discourage the insects. At this time, the herds may be huge, with thousands upon thousands of caribou traveling together.

By late July and in August, the large groups of caribou break up again into smaller herds, this time feasting upon tree leaves and other plants. Now they restore their bodies' supplies of fat and protein for the coming winter. When the first heavy snowfalls arrive in the autumn, the caribou are again on the move toward the south, using much the same routes they traveled during the spring.

Both the cows and the bulls have antlers, but the antlers are much larger and more important for the male. The spread of a bull's antlers may equal its height—four feet. The males use their antlers to twist and shove at each other, to show their strength and establish their territory. A territory holder is often so busy fighting off other males that he has no time to eat and grows weaker and weaker. Finally he may be forced off by a stronger bull, which takes over his territory. The stronger animal will then breed with the females.

Caribou need to move to find food and to survive in the harsh surroundings in which they live. During the caribou year, there are only a few weeks when these mammals are not on the march from one place to another.

Shortly after they are born, baby squirrels, rats, mice, and other small mammals set off on one-way expeditions from their birthplaces in search of food. Most of these trips are not very long, perhaps only a mile or two. But in proportion to the size of these tiny animals, the distance is the equal of a hundred-mile walk for a human.

Perhaps the best-known of all small travelers are the lemmings of the Arctic lands. Lemmings are small rodents related to meadow mice and voles. The Norwegian lemming is found in the mountains of southern Norway through Lapland and the shores of the White Sea.

In the winter, Norwegian lemmings dwell on the rocky, snowy slopes of mountains, eating the leaves of small trees and shrubs. In the spring, the melting snows flood their underground homes, and the lemmings amble down into the meadows to eat grasses. They breed during the spring, and by July they begin to return to the mountains. When the number of lemmings is low, which is most of the time, their journeys are short and easy.

Every three to four years, however, the population of lemmings suddenly increases. Lemmings can produce a litter of up to thirteen young every three weeks. That means where there are two lemmings in an area to begin with, in two or three months there may be several hundred. Although no one is sure exactly what causes this explosion of the lemming population, it seems to be tied to a mild winter and a good summer with lots of food and few predators.

The sudden increase in the number of lemmings causes problems. There is not enough food or room for them all, so the lemmings become very aggressive toward one another and even fight to the death. Large numbers leave home to find new pastures. Many others fall prey to foxes and owls. With fewer adults around, the breeding cycle slows down, and the population declines suddenly.

Every thirty years or so, an even greater population explosion occurs. In these "lemming years," the population reaches into the millions, and huge numbers of lemmings pour into the surrounding countryside, cross farmlands, and even enter towns. They eat whatever plants they find along the way. Lemmings can swim, and many easily cross rivers and streams. Eventually, the lemmings end up on the edges of large lakes and fjords that lead to the sea.

Driven by sheer numbers, the lemmings plunge into the waters and try to swim to a distant shore. If there were no water in the way, the lemmings would just keep moving on land. The lemmings are not trying to commit suicide, but rather are attempting to escape the crowds of other lemmings. Many thousands die in the attempt. The few that succeed become pioneers in new lands and start the cycle all over again.

An adult male polar bear is the largest living land carnivore (along with the Kodiak bear). It may weigh as much as fifteen hundred pounds and reach a length of more than ten feet from nose to tail. Polar bears do not have a small home range, as do most other migrating carnivores. Instead, they live on shifting ice floes and pack ice. Polar bears travel hundreds of miles on ice drifts and over snowy lands that all look alike, but somehow the bears know where they are. They do not travel aimlessly.

A female polar bear digs a den in the ice in November and gives birth to one or two cubs in December. Polar bear cubs are tiny, born hairless and helpless, each weighing only about one pound. The cubs, however, grow quickly; by March they weigh around twenty-five pounds. The mother pushes her nose through the snow, and she and her cubs go on the hunt for food. The mother has not eaten since the previous autumn, living off only her body fat. In the past six months she has lost half of her summer weight and looks gaunt.

For the rest of the spring and summer, the mother and her cubs will travel miles each day hunting for seals. The mother bear will wait on the ice alongside a seal's breathing hole. When the seal comes up for a breath of air, the bear hits out with her forearm, stuns the seal, and seizes it in her jaws. Then she and her cubs share in the meal.

Elephants are the largest land animals in the world. A male African elephant stands a dozen feet high and weighs as much as eight tons, more than the weight of a hundred children and adult humans put together. Every day an adult elephant eats about five hundred pounds of food and drinks about forty gallons of water.

Elephants spend three-quarters of the day and night eating leaves, fruit, grasses, and the bark of trees, or moving toward a new source of food. The rest of the time they spend bathing in water or mud, drinking, resting, and sleeping. A herd usually stays in one area for a few days before it moves on to find more food and water.

At one time in the past, African elephants migrated over vast distances of hundreds of miles each year, following the seasonal rains from place to place. But elephants are now found mostly in nature reserves. Their movements within a particular feeding range now follow a loop or a circle of ten to twenty miles.

The leader of a herd of elephants is usually the oldest female in the group. In a herd of fifty or more, there are a number of females and their offspring but no adult male elephants. Males stay with their families until they are about thirteen years old. Then they are usually driven away by older females of the herd.

In the dry season, May through November, mixed groups of young male and female elephant herds gather around lakes, water holes, swamps, and marshes. In the wooded areas nearby, they pluck shoots off trees with the two fingerlike lips on their trunks. They also use their trunks to uproot whole trees, to get to the high branches they couldn't otherwise reach, and they rip up the bark with their tusks and dig up roots to get more food. Elephants also need the salt and minerals that they get from salt licks—dried-up water and mud holes where the salt content in the soil is high.

Despite its thickness, an elephant's skin is very sensitive. A coating of mud, or of dust in the dry season, is a protection from insect bites and sunburn. The elephant's sensitive skin and its sharp sense of smell allow it to detect wind direction and possibly pollen and chemical cues released by growing plants. These smells may play a part in determining which direction the elephant will travel.

When the rains begin, grasses quickly sprout on the open plains and elephants start on a seasonal hundred-mile or longer journey to their wet-season feeding grounds. Migrating elephants travel single file, about as fast as a person can walk. The female family groups keep together like silent gray mounds, touching each other with their trunks and nudging the babies back into line.

By the time they reach the green, swampy plains, these herds have been joined by other groups of elephants, including adult males. The plains offer plenty of food and water, and the elephants feast on the new grasses and wallow in mud. Sometimes they give themselves showers with water sucked up into their trunks.

The rainy season is the time for elephants to mate and for babies to be born. An elephant mother stays pregnant for twenty-two months, and when her baby is born it weighs about two hundred pounds. After trying for one or two hours to stand up, the baby is able to walk and shelters itself beneath its mother's belly. It remains close to its mother for two or three more years, learning how to behave and what to eat. Elephants continue to grow all their lives and may live for fifty or sixty years or even longer.

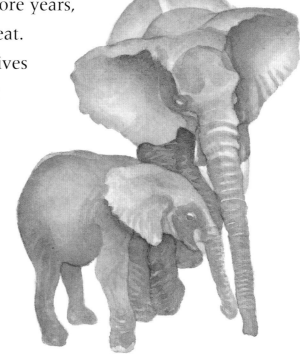

Elephants travel the same paths year after year, following along a river or going through a valley. They also seem to be able to navigate using the sun and the stars, as well as distant landmarks such as mountains. But all over the world, elephants are losing the lands they once traveled to people who have moved in to farm and to hunt. Humans are the elephants' only natural enemy. For elephants to survive, we have to set aside enough land so that they can find food in both rainy and dry seasons. Otherwise there will come a time when the only elephants left will be the ones we see in zoos and circuses.

$\mathcal{T}$hree hundred years ago, bison roamed the plains of North America in vast herds of millions of animals. A single herd of bison could cover an area twenty-five miles wide and fifty miles deep, bigger than the entire city of New York. The total number of bison in America at that time is thought to have been sixty million. These were the largest herds of big animals ever seen. They migrated in circular paths of several hundred miles between winter and summer ranges.

The Native Americans who lived on the plains relied on the vast herds of migrating bison, also called buffalo, for their survival. They made robes and tents of the buffalo's hide. They ate the meat and burned the dung for heat. The early western European settlers also depended upon the animal for food, shelter, clothing, and even heat.

But later, white hunters slaughtered the bison—apparently for sport—in huge numbers. By the beginning of the twentieth century, there were only about three hundred bison left in the United States. Today the animals live in protected sites in Yellowstone Park and other places, and their numbers have grown to more than thirty thousand.

The Lapps, also called Sámi, are nomads—wandering people—who live in the northern parts of Norway, in a region called Lapland. In April of each year, one group of Sámi begins to leave their southerly winter homes among the sheltering forests along the border of Finland. They and their herds of reindeer set off on a two-week journey to summer homes 250 miles away on the coast of the Arctic Ocean. They spend the summer there and return south in September or October.

Migrations of this kind are common among nomads who raise grazing animals. Some Bedouin of the Arabian peninsula follow shifting rainfall and pasturelands over a six-hundred-mile circuit annually. The cattle-herding Fula people of West Africa travel between dry- and wet-season homes each year.

Early humans were mostly hunter-gatherers—people who hunted game and gathered fruit and vegetables growing wild. Several hundred thousand years ago, some early humans left their original homes in East Africa and spread across Europe and southern Asia.

The development—about twelve thousand years ago—of farming and the raising of domestic animals allowed people to have a more stable existence. Still, for many peoples of the world, migrations are a constant part of life.

MORE ABOUT LAND JOURNEYS

*M*igration is sometimes thought of as a to-and-fro movement of animals from one region to another, usually connected to the change of seasons. But the word actually covers a wide variety of animal travels. Some animals migrate many times within their life span, while others migrate only once.

Some migrations cover hundreds or thousands of miles; others take place within a mile or two of the animal's birthplace. Permanent movements of animals away from their birthplaces are sometimes called emigrations. Wandering from one place to another to find food is sometimes called nomadism.

But some scientists now think that migration, emigration, and nomadism are just a few of the ways that particular species of animals survive in nature. Rather than trying to apply a label to the kind of life-journeys animals take, these scientists prefer to explain and describe what happens in an animal's life.

Perhaps the first overland journeys ever attempted by animals took place four hundred million years ago, when the earliest amphibians crawled from the dark waters of ancient seas onto the wet mudflats of new land. Nowadays most amphibians, such as frogs, toads, and salamanders, repeat that original trip as part of their life cycle.

Amphibians spend most of their lives on land, but they must return to a pond, lake, or stream to lay their eggs. The larvae or tadpoles hatch and then spend from a few weeks to two or three years in the water. While they live and develop in the water, they get oxygen through their gills. Later, amphibians develop lungs, breathe air, and change into small adults before journeying onto land.

The distances that frogs and salamanders cover is not great compared to the travels of many other animals—a few miles at most. But their journeys are among the most dangerous. Unlike most mammals, amphibians are not well suited for their overland travels. They have moist, smooth skin without the protection of hair, scales, or feathers. If an amphibian is exposed to the heat of the sun or its skin dries up for even a few minutes, it will die.

Most amphibians are also small. When they leave the water to live on land, they become vulnerable to all kinds of predators, including birds, snakes, foxes, wild cats, and other animals. Modern life has created another danger for the small travelers. Thousands of frogs and toads are killed every year by cars traveling on roads that lie between the amphibians' land homes and the ponds and lakes where they breed.

Each amphibian has its own particular difficult journey, but the life cycles of common pond frogs of the Americas and Europe are typical of many species. In late winter these frogs emerge from hollows in rotting logs or from leaf-covered holes in the ground where they have spent the winter protected from both predators and bad weather.

Bulging with eggs, the female hops to a nearby pond to find a mate. She lays her eggs in the water and the male fertilizes the eggs as they emerge. Each female lays between fifteen hundred and three thousand eggs within a few seconds. A jellylike material covers each egg and swells on contact with the water. The eggs float in large masses near the surface, each with its developing embryo. Neither parent takes any further interest in its offspring.

As the embryos develop, they begin to look more and more like tadpoles. In two weeks, the tiny tadpoles struggle free of the jelly, and within a few days they begin feeding on weeds and algae in the water. The young tadpoles are hunted by dragonfly nymphs, diving beetles, and other insects, fish, and even other frogs. Only a few are lucky enough to survive.

After several weeks the tadpoles develop lungs, then hind legs, and then front legs. In less than two months, the change from tadpole to frog is complete. The young frogs leave the water, switching from a plant diet to one of insects. They live around the edges of the pond until it is time to hibernate in the winter. Not until they are two or three years old will they make the dangerous journeys far from the water and then back to the pond to spawn.

Bears, wolves, foxes, and lynxes are carnivores—hunters that feed upon other animals. Carnivores need to follow the movements of their prey, and if their prey migrates vast distances, then the carnivores also travel long distances in their search for food.

Two hundred years ago, wolf packs probably followed the huge herds of bison that roamed the Great Plains of North America. Now they follow migrating herds of caribou for hundreds of miles across the treeless arctic tundra.

The Canadian lynx, a big cat, usually has a home territory where it hunts the snowshoe and the arctic hare. In good years prey is very plentiful and the lynx does not have to travel very far to find food. But every nine or ten years the population of hares suddenly drops, and the hungry lynx has to wander far from its normal range. It may travel hundreds of miles to find prey.

Bears also may travel long distances when prey or other food supplies are not available. When drought destroyed a berry crop in Minnesota one spring, a young black bear traveled through fields and farmlands to an oak forest area 125 miles away. He stayed there until October, when it was time to return home to his den.

The bear moved at night, avoiding settled areas and barking dogs. He was on an unfamiliar route, but he seemed to know his way, moving directly homeward under clear or cloudy skies. In some strange fashion we don't understand, bears seem to be able to follow a compass in their heads. Finally, the bear found his way back to his home territory and entered a rocky den to spend the winter.

A migratory herd of large animals was a welcome sight for the humans living on the northern plains during the last Ice Age. Bison, horses, mammoths, caribou, and antelope wandered past our ancestors' shelters, following migratory routes. With the arrival of the herds came food and clothing and a chance to store up supplies for the winter.

Most of these animals are no longer present in the huge numbers that once roamed the plains of North America, Europe, and Asia. Some, such as the woolly mammoth, are extinct. Others, such as the European bison and Przewalski's horse (a small wild horse found in Mongolia), are near extinction.

The only plains animal left in sizable herds outside Africa is the saiga, a kind of Asian antelope that migrates between the Caspian Sea and Mongolia. The saiga's trunklike nose warms air up before it reaches the lungs. For centuries, the saiga was hunted for food and clothing. But hunters using guns sharply reduced the numbers of saigas so that there were only a thousand animals left at the beginning of the twentieth century. Laws were passed protecting the saigas, and their numbers have grown.

Until the late nineteenth century, springbok—small antelope—were found in the millions in the plains of South Africa. One herd was estimated to be 130 miles long and 12 miles wide, containing a million animals. But the springbok competed with the settlers' domestic grazing animals for food. So the springbok were hunted, and the huge herds were destroyed. The tiny number of springbok that are still left live on nature reserves.

The illustrations in this book were done in watercolor on
Fabriano Artistico, 140 lb. cold-press, 100%-cotton paper.
The display type was set in Pietra.
The text type was set in Meridien Medium.
Color separations by Bright Arts Ltd., Hong Kong
Printed by South China Printing Company, Ltd., Hong Kong
This book was printed on totally chlorine-free Nymolla Matte Art paper.
Production supervision by Stanley Redfern
Designed by Judythe Sieck